DATE DUE		

Mikhail Gorbachev

JUNIOR ▪ WORLD ▪ BIOGRAPHIES

Mikhail Gorbachev

JOHN W. SELFRIDGE

CHELSEA JUNIORS

a division of CHELSEA HOUSE PUBLISHERS

Chelsea House Publishers
EDITOR-IN-CHIEF: Remmel Nunn
MANAGING EDITOR: Karyn Gullen Browne
COPY CHIEF: Juliann Barbato
PICTURE EDITOR: Adrian G. Allen
ART DIRECTOR: Maria Epes
DEPUTY COPY CHIEF: Mark Rifkin
ASSISTANT ART DIRECTOR: Noreen Romano
MANUFACTURING MANAGER: Gerald Levine
SYSTEMS MANAGER: Lindsey Ottman
PRODUCTION MANAGER: Joseph Romano
PRODUCTION COORDINATOR: Marie Claire Cebrián

JUNIOR WORLD BIOGRAPHIES

EDITOR: Remmel Nunn

Staff for MIKHAIL GORBACHEV
COPY EDITOR: Benson Simmonds
PICTURE RESEARCHERS: Brian Araujo, Jonathan Shapiro
SENIOR DESIGNER: Marjorie Zaum
COVER ILLUSTRATOR: Kye Carbonne

First Printing

1 3 5 7 9 8 6 4 2

Library of Congress Cataloging-in-Publication Data
Selfridge, John W.
  Mikhail Gorbachev/John W. Selfridge
    p. cm.—(Junior world biographies)
  Summary: A biography of the leader of the Soviet Union.
  ISBN 0-7910-1567-X
  1. Gorbachev, Mikhail Sergeevich, 1931– —Juvenile
literature. 2. Heads of state—Soviet Union—Biography—Juvenile
literature. [1. Gorbachev, Mikhail Sergeevich, 1931– . 2. Heads of state.]
I. Title. II. Series.   90-49471
DK290.3.G67S45 1992   CIP
[92]—dc20   AC

Contents

Mikhail Gorbachev responds to a cheering crowd with a smile and a gesture of unity in 1987. During his visit to the United States that year, the Soviet leader won the hearts of many Americans with his warm personality.

1

"Gorbymania!"

On the last day of his visit to the United States in December 1987, Mikhail Gorbachev was feeling great. He had spent several days meeting with high officials of the U.S. government, including President Ronald Reagan. Gorbachev and Reagan had overcome differences that had seemed impossible to resolve and that had divided their two countries since World War II. After two failed meetings in Switzerland and Iceland, Gorbachev and Reagan had reached an understanding and signed a historic treaty banning short- and middle-range nuclear missiles on both sides. It was the first treaty designed to eliminate an entire category of nuclear missiles.

As his motorcade moved through the streets of Washington, D.C., Gorbachev looked through the dark glass window of his limousine and saw the cheering crowds that had turned out to wish him well. His visit to the United States had been an astounding success. He had signed a treaty aimed at bringing the world one step closer to lasting peace. He had also won the hearts of the American people with his warmth, honesty, and intelligence. Most important, he had set the tone of world politics for many years to come.

Gorbachev did not look like the great world leader or the celebrity he had become. He was short, stocky, and balding, his gray hair no longer covering the unusual red birthmark on the top of his head. Because he suffered from back problems, his movements were stiff. Like the Soviet leaders before him, he usually wore a conservative gray or dark blue suit with the Communist party insignia pinned to his wide lapel. Looking at the man, nobody would have thought that he would redefine world politics and become an adored international personality. But his eyes, his smile, and, most of all, his message had made the difference.

Now he was being driven to the White House, for one last meeting with President Reagan before returning home. The street was filled with people craning to catch a glimpse of him. Why not stop, he thought, get out of the car, and greet these people face-to-face?

When Gorbachev ordered him to stop the car, the driver was shocked and did so with a jolt, believing there must be something wrong. After all, why would Secretary Gorbachev order the car to be stopped if everything was fine? Some of the drivers farther ahead in the motorcade were slow to realize that Gorbachev's car had stopped. When they did, they almost panicked. There must be a problem, they thought. Was Secretary Gorbachev's life in danger? They hurriedly backed up to join the main car.

The Soviet KGB and U.S. Secret Service men assigned to protect the Soviet delegation were thrown into a frenzy as the door of Gorbachev's car opened. They could not believe their eyes when a smiling Gorbachev stepped out of the car and mingled with the cheering masses. "I want to say hello to you," he told the adoring crowd, and he proceeded to shake as many hands as he could, grinning and waving before being urged back into the car by concerned Secret Service men.

Never had a Soviet leader seemed so friendly and sincere. And certainly never before had a Soviet leader suddenly emerged from the safety of his bulletproof limousine to meet and speak with people in the streets. But this was Mikhail Gorbachev, the man who in a relatively short time had brought extraordinarily liberal social and political changes to his country. Where there was once secrecy, there was now openness; where there had been fear and frustration, there was now an eagerness to speak out and work together. Where before the future was dark, there was now enthusiasm and hope. And Gorbachev had done more than restructure systems within the Soviet Union's borders. He had brought the country back into the world community with a spirit of cooperation rarely seen in the international political arena. He was a man of the people, and he wanted to take his message directly to them.

Who was this man Mikhail Gorbachev? Where did he get his revolutionary ideas? How has he been able to be so successful in such dramatic ways in so short a time? And what are his goals for the future? To answer these questions, we will begin our story in a seemingly unlikely place—a small, isolated Russian peasant village in the 1930s.

Russian peasants take a break from their farm labors to share a drink and a song. Despite the harsh Russian climate and short growing season, the Soviet economy is agriculturally based.

2

The Growth of a Nation

Mikhail Sergeevich Gorbachev, or "Misha," as his parents Sergei and Maria Gorbachev called him, was born on March 2, 1931, in the small Russian town of Privolnoye, in the region called Stavropol. Eight hundred miles south of the city of Moscow, Privolnoye was not a place where one might expect a great world political leader to be born. Most people there were illiterate farmers, like their fathers and like their fathers before them. Mikhail's parents were farmers, as were his grandparents.

When Mikhail Gorbachev was born, the leader of the Soviet Union was Joseph Stalin. At the time, Stalin was loved and respected by the Soviet people, but his policies slowly led to disaster. Mikhail grew up as this disaster was beginning, but he was taught that Stalin had saved Russia from an even worse fate.

For centuries, he learned, the vast Russian farmland was worked by hired laborers called serfs. From season to season, the serfs planted and harvested crops for the landowners, who then gave the serfs barely enough food to survive. The landowners then sold or kept the crops for themselves and their families. As a result, a serf's life was little better than that of a slave. In 1861, the government set the serfs free by giving these poor farm laborers small plots of land of their own to work. This way they themselves, rather than the wealthy landlords, could enjoy or sell the fruits of their own labor.

Though by no means perfect, this new system improved the lives of the former serfs. As

Ukrainian peasants work the fields. Lenin found the Russian peasantry extremely conservative; his attempts to modernize the country's farming methods met with mass resistance.

peasant farmers on their own land, they were able to feed themselves and their families and still have something to sell to people in the cities. Even so, many peasant farmers continued to struggle and remained poor.

In 1917, there was a revolution in Russia, and a man named Vladimir Ilyich Ulyanov, or Lenin as he was called, became the leader of Russia, now called the Soviet Union. Lenin tried to help the peasants improve their lot even further by giving them more land. When Lenin died, however, Stalin took his place and tried to reverse Lenin's plan. He joined the small farms together to make larger farms run by the government. This was called farm collectivization.

Stalin believed strongly in government control and was sure that more and better food would be produced on government-run farms. But the peasant farmers disagreed. They wanted to remain free of government control, even if it meant they would continue to be poor. So, they resisted Stalin's plan.

Stalin was not a patient man and would not put up with anyone who disagreed with him. On his orders, many of the farmers who wanted to remain free were forced to leave the country, others were thrown in jail, and still others were killed. With so many farmers forced from their land, small farms throughout the Soviet Union fell to ruin and the larger farms were unable to meet the country's demand for food. As a result, millions of people starved.

Lenin's successor, Joseph Stalin, refused to tolerate resistance to his programs. His stubborn attempt to bring the country's farms under state control met with fierce opposition and resulted in starvation and economic disaster for the Russian peasantry.

Mikhail and his family were more fortunate. Because his grandfather did not resist collectivization, and because his father took a job working on a government-owned farm, the family survived. Mikhail was able to start school at the age of eight and lived from day to day with little fear. Still, he saw many of his friends and neighbors forced off their land, imprisoned, and even killed by the government. The Gorbachevs, though members of the Soviet Union's ruling Communist party, were not without worries.

Eventually, because of the failure of his farm collectivization policy, Stalin became worried that the Soviet people would force him out of power. He became so worried that he began to imagine enemies all around him. Throughout the 1930s, Stalin ordered the killing of hundreds of thousands of people whom he thought he could not trust. Those who were spared were sent to prison camps in Siberia, a cold, dreary region in eastern Russia. In Siberia they were poorly fed, given meager shelter, and forced to do heavy manual labor.

During the 1940s, the Soviet Union experienced continued hardship. In 1941, it was invaded by Germany, which was then ruled by Adolf Hitler. Hitler, whose ideas were based on hatred and a belief in the superior strength of the German military, wanted to rule the world. Hitler's forces and those of his allies, Japan and Italy, clashed with the armies of the United States, Great Britain, France, and the Soviet Union. Because it involved so many nations, the conflict was called World War II.

Though German forces never reached his hometown, the war had a powerful effect on Mikhail Gorbachev's life. His school, like many schools in the Soviet Union during the war, was closed. And when his father joined the Soviet army to fight the Germans, the family's money soon began to run out. When the school was re-opened, Mikhail could not return because his mother did not have enough money to buy him shoes. Eventually, however, she was able to, and Mikhail returned to his studies. Happy to be back in school, he proved to be an excellent student, winning several important scholastic awards.

During the four years his father was fighting in the war, Gorbachev grew into an emotionally and intellectually intense young man. He worked on the family farm even while keeping up with his studies and walking 12 miles to and from school each day. He read a lot, especially poetry and fiction, and became known to his peers as a young intellectual. The older townspeople of Privolnoye, many of whom could not read or write, often asked Mikhail to read them the daily newspaper. When he did, conversation usually followed. They would discuss political issues, and the young Gorbachev was not shy about voicing his opinions. He loved to debate and did so with

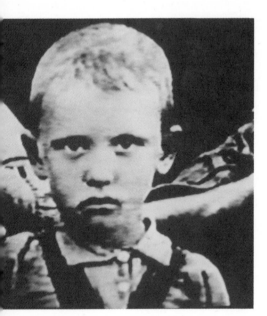

Mikhail Gorbachev grew up during the Stalin era. Thus, as a boy he experienced the strife brought on by Stalin's plans during the 1930s and by the hardships of World War II during the 1940s, when Germany invaded the Soviet Union.

everyone who would grapple with him. For Gorbachev, who had very strong opinions, there was nothing more satisfying than successfully defending one's position. His classmates soon learned that in the art of argument, Mikhail Gorbachev was without equal.

While Mikhail was getting his education, the Soviet army was fighting to drive the Germans out of Russia, which they finally did in 1943. World War II ended two years later, when Japan, Italy, and Germany were finally defeated.

But the Soviet Union had lost 20 million lives in the war, more than any other country. Many of its cities had been bombed and burned. Seeing his country in such a sad state, Mikhail Gorbachev, now 14, was stirred with the desire to help rebuild it. He began working as a farm machine operator after school and during the summer. He also became politically active by joining the Komsomol, a Communist youth organization dedicated to grooming future members of the Communist party.

Though the Communist party is the only political party in the Soviet Union, not everyone can become a member. To do so, one must apply and be accepted. Only a select few are accepted for party membership, and even then, acceptance is only on a one-year trial basis. In the Soviet Union, one cannot take part in government decisions, nor can one hope to rise to the top of a profession without first being accepted as a member of the party.

Gorbachev applied for party membership in 1950. He had high hopes of being accepted because he had proven himself to be a hard worker, a bright student, and a devoted member of the Komsomol. He had the support of several local party officials. Also, his father and grandfather were party members.

Around this time, Gorbachev also applied for admission to college. A relatively small number of students are accepted into the few Soviet colleges each year, so the Gorbachevs, and everyone else in Privolnoye, celebrated when they learned that their Misha was accepted at Moscow State University. To enter such a school was a great privilege, especially for someone from a peasant family.

Selecting a field of study is no easy matter for a young college student. After much thought, Gorbachev chose law because of his growing interest in politics and government. He worked hard and impressed his teachers. In 1952, he was accepted as a member of the Communist party.

Though students often poked fun at Gorbachev for his rough peasant manners and way of speaking, some found him a very interesting schoolmate. In particular, Gorbachev's roommate, Zdenek Mlynar, took a liking to his friend from Privolnoye. Mlynar was from Czechoslovakia, a central European country under Soviet rule. The two often went to films and plays together. They talked about history, literature, music, and most of all politics. Mlynar admired Gorbachev's honesty, loyalty, leadership qualities, and natural intelligence. From Mlynar, Gorbachev learned about the world outside of the Soviet Union, especially about Czechoslovakia, a country that had known very difficult times in its history.

Another student at the college took a liking to Gorbachev. Raisa Titorenko, a student of philosophy, was two years younger than Gorbachev. She was born in Siberia, where her father was a railroad worker, but later moved with her family to the Stavropol region where she, like Gorbachev, grew up. The two met in a dance class at the college and were happy to discover that they lived in the same college dormitory.

Their friendship became romantic even though dormitory life was difficult for young lovers. There was almost no privacy. Thousands of students lived at the college, and as many as eight shared each room. The dormitory had no bathtubs; students had to take baths at public bathhouses and could do so only two or three times a month. And the workload at the college left students with little time for socializing. Still, Mikhail and Raisa saw each other whenever they could.

Their relationship deepened, and finally they were married in 1954, Gorbachev's senior year. The newlyweds moved into a university-owned building for married students. They still had only a single room for themselves, but at least they were together.

By the time Gorbachev was ready to graduate from the university in 1955, he had sharpened the skills that would help him in his future political career. Especially good at public speaking, Gorbachev became a leading Komsomol organizer and secretary to the law faculty. But he had also become a good listener, having learned the value of the thoughts and opinions of others.

After a disappointing job search in Moscow, Gorbachev and Raisa decided to leave the city and return to Stavropol. From there Mikhail would start his climb to the top of the Soviet government.

A *huge bucket of molten metal is transported by a powerful crane at a Soviet steel mill. During his years in power, Stalin was determined to industrialize the Soviet economy, even if it cost the lives of millions of peasants.*

3

The Long Climb
to the Top

In 1955, Gorbachev took a position as secretary of the local Komsomol in Stavropol and then worked as the Komsomol's deputy chief of propaganda, speaking to young people at meetings, in schools, and in factories. Raisa Gorbachev got a job as a schoolteacher. The Gorbachevs felt good about returning to the region of their childhood.

But Stavropol was not Moscow, and the Gorbachevs missed the excitement of the big city. Mikhail Gorbachev hoped that it would not be long before he landed a high post in the Soviet government and he and Raisa could move back to Moscow. Little did he know it would take 23 years for that to happen.

Promotions, however, came easily to Gorbachev during those years. He became first secretary of the Stavropol Komsomol—the highest political position in the city—when he was only 27 years old. But Gorbachev still felt he was ready for greater responsibility.

Fyodor Kulakov also thought Gorbachev was ready. Kulakov had held an important post in the Soviet national government but had lost his job under Soviet leader Nikita Khrushchev. He took a post in the Stavropol region in 1960 and worked closely with Gorbachev. The two became very good friends. When Khrushchev was replaced by Leonid Brezhnev in 1964, Kulakov returned to the national government. Thus, Gorbachev suddenly had a friend in a high place.

Things were also going very well for the Gorbachevs in Stavropol. In 1956, Raisa had given birth to a daughter, Irina, and had gone back to school for an advanced degree. In 1967, she received her doctorate in sociology from the Lenin Institute in Moscow. By this time, Mikhail too had earned a graduate degree, in agricultural economics.

Meanwhile, Mikhail was learning more and more about how to be a politician. He walked to work every day, always finding time to chat with people along his way. He listened closely to their problems and complaints, and though he made no promises, he did what he could to help the average citizen. He also began to understand the value of the press and how a politician can use the press to his advantage. In 1970, he became first secretary of the Communist party for the entire Stavropol region. Then, in 1971, he was named a member of the Central Committee of the Communist party of the Soviet Union.

Things were not going so well for the Soviet Union, however. Under Brezhnev, the Soviet economy was becoming weak, and because unqualified people were given high positions, nobody with power really knew how to run the government. Unemployment and alcoholism poisoned the nation's outlook. The Soviet people were losing hope. One man who really wanted to do something to help his country was Yuri Andropov.

Soviet leader Nikita Khrushchev chats with workers on a collective farm in 1956. Under Khrushchev, Soviet farmers learned new methods, and harvest yields improved.

Andropov was head of the KGB, the Soviet Union's national police force. He had many ideas on how to solve the country's problems, but because he had kidney trouble and diabetes he was not healthy enough to act on them. At about this time, Andropov visited a spa, where he regularly took baths in mineral water, hoping that doing so would improve his health. The spa that Andropov visited was in the Stavropol region, and this proved very lucky for Gorbachev.

When Gorbachev met Andropov to greet him to the region, the two liked each other right away. Andropov, somewhat shy, felt comfortable in the company of Gorbachev, who was very warm and friendly. He impressed the KGB leader with his intelligence and perfect manners. Mrs. Andropov also took a liking to Raisa Gorbachev, and the two began to take regular walks together. Eventually, the four of them were the best of friends.

As Mikhail Gorbachev gained another friend in a high place by spending time with Andropov, he lost one as well. In July 1978, Fyodor Kulakov died of a heart attack. Gorbachev spoke at Kulakov's funeral, which was broadcast over Soviet television and radio. Thus, citizens throughout the Soviet Union got to see and hear Gorbachev for the first time. Many of them knew right away that this man from Stavropol was something special.

Andropov, who already knew that Gorbachev was something special, suggested to Brezhnev that he consider replacing Kulakov with Gorbachev as secretary of agriculture of the party's Central Committee. He argued that Gorbachev was young, bright, and had a very strong record at the local-government level. Brezhnev considered Gorbachev young and inexperienced, but he agreed to meet him before making up his mind. After their meeting, Brezhnev agreed to Andropov's proposal, and Gorbachev, at age 47, was offered the job. He was suddenly one of the most powerful people in the Soviet Union.

The Gorbachevs were thrilled to return to Moscow. Raisa Gorbachev took a teaching position in the philosophy department of Moscow State University, where she had gone to college. Irina Gorbachev, who had been studying medicine in Moscow, was now married and expecting a baby. And, of course, Mikhail Gorbachev was now walking the halls of the Kremlin, the huge fortress that houses the government of the Soviet Union.

Even though Gorbachev was excited about his new powerful position, he knew very well that his job as head of agriculture would be a difficult one. Crops may be grown on only 10 percent of the Soviet Union's land because the climate throughout most of the country is too harsh. The Soviet Union relied heavily on imported grain and meat, and there was not always enough food to feed all the Soviet people. Gorbachev thus faced the same problems the country had faced for centuries.

The problems proved too great even for Gorbachev. The 1979 and 1980 harvests were poor. But Gorbachev was not blamed for the crop failures, which were really the result of very bad weather. Soviet leaders felt Gorbachev had done his best, and in 1980 they made him a full member of the Politburo, the Soviet Union's ruling government body. Thus, Gorbachev, now 49, became the Politburo's youngest member. In fact, he was 20 years younger than the average age of the other 14 members.

Finally, Gorbachev felt his career was moving quickly and in the right direction. But things soon became uncertain. The aging Brezhnev was ill, and there was a power struggle among his possible replacements, especially between the two most likely candidates, Konstantin Chernenko and Yuri Andropov. Gorbachev knew that his future would be in the hands of whoever replaced Brezhnev, so he watched the political developments in Moscow very closely. When his old friend Andropov won the power struggle and was elected general secretary, Gorbachev was happy. His future looked very bright.

And how bright it was! The next step for Gorbachev came a few months later. Andropov's health began to fail, and he needed an aide to help him carry out his duties abroad. He chose Gorbachev, who had always had a keen interest in other cultures and in visiting other countries. Gorbachev, who had taken his first trip abroad—to France—in 1969, believed that the solutions to many of his country's problems could be found by studying the social, political, economic, and industrial systems of other nations. So, he was eager to travel.

In 1983, Gorbachev went to Canada. There he visited the country's factories and farms and met with Canadian leaders. Always very curious, he asked them many questions about the Canadian way of life, and they asked him many questions as well. Unlike previous Soviet leaders, who never admitted their country's own shortcomings and failures and always tried to avoid answering tough questions, Gorbachev gave truthful answers to even the hardest questions. This greatly impressed the Canadians. Likewise, from the Canadians Gorbachev learned a great deal about what might be done to improve conditions in the Soviet Union.

A year later, Yuri Andropov died of kidney failure, and Konstantin Chernenko once more eyed the job of general secretary. But now so did Gorbachev. Chernenko was 72 years old, had little experience in agriculture or industry management, and was not well educated. Gorbachev was young and energetic, extremely bright, and a proven manager in the agricultural area. But Chernenko's many close friends in the Soviet government wanted a friend at the top who would not change things that much. Their chief concern was for their own jobs. Gorbachev, a relative newcomer and someone likely to shake things up, was therefore denied the post.

That Chernenko's health was unsteady became obvious very quickly. At Andropov's funeral, Chernenko was barely able to finish his speech. As the parade passed, he could hardly raise his arm to salute. Gorbachev, on the other hand, showed not only his energy, serving as a pallbearer, but his warmth. When Andropov's widow, Tatyana, began to cry, the other Soviet leaders stiffly ignored her. Gorbachev put his arm around her and tried to calm her.

In the next few months Gorbachev traveled to Great Britain, where he met Prime Minister Margaret Thatcher and charmed the British public. Raisa, whom the British media called the Soviet Union's answer to Princess Diana, also impressed the English.

Back home, Chernenko was growing weaker and weaker. When he died on March 10, 1985, the Soviet people were relieved. Chernenko had been the last remaining Soviet leader from the Stalin era. It was time for a change. The Soviet Union needed a young, dynamic leader who would not be afraid to shake off the old ways and try new ideas. Mikhail Gorbachev's chance had finally come.

Soviet leader Gorbachev chats with Romanian students during a visit to Bucharest, their country's capital. His wife, Raisa, is at his side.

CHAPTER

4

The New Man in Charge

Gorbachev was elected general secretary of the Communist party of the Soviet Union at an emergency Politburo meeting in March 1985. In his acceptance speech, Gorbachev wasted no time before making changes. He said he intended to open up the Soviet economy to new kinds of growth possibilities by allowing some factories and farms to be privately owned. He also said he wanted people to express their views publicly, to participate in their government, and to travel abroad.

These goals troubled many of the older members of the Politburo. The kinds of changes Gorbachev was hoping to make were drastic. In the Soviet Union, a Communist country, there was no such thing as private factories and farms. In a Communist system, everything belongs to the state. Also, the Soviet Union had long been a "closed society," where opinions were not aired publicly unless approved by the government, where only Communist party members participated in government, and where getting a passport or a visa was very difficult if not impossible. By saying he wanted to change all this, Gorbachev scared the "old guard," the conservative men in the Politburo, who knew that they would lose their hold on power in a more open society. The Soviet people, however, were for the most part overjoyed.

Aware that the Politburo would resist his changes and possibly seek his removal, Gorbachev was careful not to move too quickly. Shrewdly, he prepared the ground for the seeds of change.

He appointed many new party members to replace the old ones, to be sure that he had a majority of support in the Politburo. Now he knew he could get things done with less resistance.

Sensing that the time was right, Gorbachev introduced important changes to spur economic growth in the Soviet Union. He put in place a system in which workers were rewarded with cash bonuses for especially hard work. By lessening government restrictions, he gave farm owners more freedom to manage their farms and the ability to earn more from them. In an effort to encourage growth in all areas, he introduced computers to the Soviet Union, which had been slow to develop such electronic technology except for very special purposes.

The most astonishing change that Gorbachev made was the encouragement of public debate. Seeking public support for his new policies, Gorbachev took his message directly to the people. This had not been done by a Soviet leader since Lenin. Gorbachev visited homes, farms, factories, and hospitals to seek advice from Soviet citizens. He urged them to be frank with him, to tell him their problems, and to let him know how things might be changed for the better. In a country where for decades one could end up in jail for criticizing the government, Gorbachev now told the people to talk not only among themselves but to journalists and directly to the country's leaders without fear of punishment.

During the Stalin era, many Soviet people were imprisoned or lost their lives for voicing their opinions. Now, the new Soviet leader was saying that people had to be free to speak up and that it was one's duty as a citizen to do so. He called this freedom *glasnost* (openness). Although it remained illegal to criticize the KGB, the Soviet military, or high-ranking government officials, the Soviet people suddenly had a voice and the power to change public policy.

The effect of glasnost on Soviet society was tremendous. People began discussing issues in public that previously would have to be discussed only at home, if at all. Newspaper reporters began to investigate Soviet social problems and to publish their findings. People began to read books that had previously been banned from publication by the government. Writers, artists, musicians, and filmmakers all enjoyed their newfound freedom. Even rock music, previously banned, was now allowed.

Gorbachev then launched an attack on one of the Soviet Union's most dire social problems—alcoholism. Because the Soviet life had been difficult for so many for so long, an increasing number of Soviet people, bored and depressed, had turned to alcohol to forget their troubles. Although drinking beer and liquor is popular in many countries, Gorbachev realized that the Soviet people were drinking too much and for the wrong reasons. It was estimated that there were some 9 million alcoholics in the Soviet Union, many of whom admitted to drinking liquor, usually vodka, before work or on the job, and that this problem cost the country $8 billion in lost productivity, increased crime, car accidents, and additional health care.

Such a waste, Gorbachev believed, should not be the fate of a great people. So, he set about passing laws aimed at curbing alcohol abuse. He raised the minimum drinking age from 18 to 21 and passed a law that prohibited restaurants from selling more than two drinks with a single meal. The selling of alcohol before 2:00 in the afternoon was also prohibited. People found drunk in public or on the job were fined or jailed, and alcohol was no longer served at government meetings.

Gorbachev's antialcohol campaign met with mixed reviews. Alcohol is an addictive drug, meaning that those who use it regularly can grow physically dependent on it. Many Soviet citizens, unable to face life without vodka, spent their days in lines in front of liquor stores. Others began making their own liquor at home, without expert knowledge and government regulation. As a result, a black market in liquor got started, and many people became seriously ill from drinking homemade vodka. Despite these unfortunate developments, the Soviet Union saw a marked increase in worker productivity as a result of Gorbachev's alcohol reforms, and many Soviet citizens were grateful for Gorbachev's efforts. Still, the Soviet leader had to ease the restrictions for the time being, realizing that simply passing laws would not solve the problem.

Gorbachev and Canada's agricultural minister inspect some Canadian wine during the Soviet leader's visit to Ottawa in 1983. For health reasons, Gorbachev does not drink alcohol.

During the summer of 1985, Gorbachev toured the Soviet Union. Everywhere he went he was a hit. His genuine warmth and plainspoken manner won the people over. His picture was on the cover of every newspaper and magazine. He was quoted frequently, as readers seemed never to get enough of Gorbachev's wisdom. He had set in motion the wheels of reform, but it remained to be seen if they would continue to turn.

With the publication of his book, *Perestroika: New Thinking for Our Country and the World*, Gorbachev outlined his goals for the future. The word *perestroika* is Russian for "restructuring," and this was what Gorbachev wanted to do—to restructure not only the economic and political system of the Soviet Union but the way in which the countries of the world relate to each other. In this way, his book was not written only for Soviet readers but for people everywhere. Before long, people the world over were reading Gorbachev's book, and his celebrity became more international.

On April 25, 1986, disaster struck—an accident at the nuclear power plant at Chernobyl, 80 miles north of the city of Kiev, in the region of the Soviet Union called the Ukraine. The results were devastating. Thirty-one people died when the Chernobyl reactor exploded, and some 6,000 people were expected to die in the future from cancer because of their exposure to the radioactivity released by the explosion. The radioactivity spread and affected neighboring countries as well, killing or contaminating animals and plant life in Poland, Sweden, Finland, and West Germany.

Despite the new openness and relatively free flow of information in the Soviet Union, a full 48 hours passed before people learned of the accident. Gorbachev disappeared for several weeks, studying the Chernobyl situation with Soviet nuclear experts. Finally, he appeared on national television to explain that the danger was over, and he dismissed the people at the plant who had neglected to follow safety regulations. A full report outlining the causes of the incident was published, and nuclear experts from outside the Soviet Union were invited and came to study the effects on the people exposed to the radiation. Such invitations would never have been extended before glasnost. Thus, though stalled in the immediate wake of the accident at Chernobyl, glasnost recovered as information became readily available to people both inside and outside the Soviet Union.

Late that year, the Soviet Union and the world continued to be astounded by Gorbachev's bold moves in the name of glasnost. He freed Soviet dissident Anatoly Scharansky, a Jew who had been in prison for nine years after being accused of spying for the United States (a charge that was never proved). Gorbachev then phoned another dissident, the Nobel Prize–winning physicist Andrei Sakharov, who seven years before had been exiled to the city of Gorky for his political views. Gorbachev invited Sakharov to end his exile and return to Moscow. Sakharov agreed to do so on the condition that Gorbachev release a number of other political prisoners. When Gorbachev accepted the condition, Sakharov was shocked and delighted, as was the international community.

But not everyone was delighted with Gorbachev. The old guard thought he was changing things too quickly. Still others thought that change was not happening fast enough. Leaders on both sides of the fence attacked Gorbachev's policies and even called for his dismissal. But Gorbachev managed to hold on to the support of the majority of the Politburo, and the Soviet people were behind him.

Still, the road ahead would be a difficult one. Conditions within the Soviet Union were very slow to improve. Despite Gorbachev's reforms, the Soviet economy remained weak, and the Soviet people, not to mention Gorbachev's rivals in the Politburo, were impatient. Also, on the horizon was perhaps an even greater challenge than fixing the Soviet economy—improving relations with the United States.

Gorbachev and U.S. president Ronald Reagan share a lighter moment during their first meeting, in Geneva, Switzerland, in 1985. The two got off to a difficult beginning, but they later became good friends.

5

Old Enemies, New Friends

Since the days of Stalin, the Soviet Union and the United States have been rivals. This is mainly because the Soviet Union is a Communist country, which means that its economic system is based on common ownership and an equal distribution of wealth. The United States, on the other hand, is a capitalist country, meaning that its economic system is based on private ownership and competition. Because of this important difference, the United States and the Soviet Union have, since the end of World War II, been engaged in what has come to be known as the *cold war*. Nearly half a century later, the ways in which these countries play the game of world politics are still often at odds.

This rivalry between the Soviet Union and the United States is of global importance because each has military strength far superior to the other nations of the world. Because they are great military powers, these two countries constantly play a major role in world politics. The *superpowers*, as these two countries came to be known, have a hand in policy decisions affecting large and small nations around the world each day.

Several factors contributed to the United States' becoming a world power. America's abundant natural resources, the ingenuity of its people, and its generally strong economy have been the most important of these factors. In its relatively short history, the United States has become one of the most important players in international business and political affairs, not only by building military might but by using its talents and resources to its best advantage in all areas of life.

The Soviet Union, however, came to be a world power mainly by building a powerful military force. Unlike its superpower rival, the Soviet Union does not have a wealth of natural resources. It has oil and minerals underground, but because of its harsh climate, very little of the Soviet Union's enormous territory can be farmed. As a result, the Soviet economy, which has always been agriculturally based, has been weak and unstable. Despite this, the Soviet Union became a superpower by putting whatever resources it had into the building of a strong military.

When Gorbachev came to power in the Soviet Union, he understood that his country was at a critical moment in its history. No longer could valuable resources be wasted on tanks and nuclear weapons. They now had to be spent on industrial development, manufacturing, business, and trade. The Soviet Union could not afford to run in an arms race with the United States, each trying to outdo the other in military might, while there was not enough food on Soviet tables. Gorbachev realized that the survival of the Soviet Union, indeed, that of the world, required that leaders lay down their arms and strive together for world peace and prosperity. Gorbachev's understanding of this was central to his vision as a great world leader.

President Ronald Reagan had a different view. He remained intent on warding off the so-called Communist threat through military might. During Reagan's eight years in office, an enormous portion of the national budget was spent on the U.S. military. Gorbachev knew that if the arms race was going to end, he was the one who had to take the initiative.

One way that Reagan was pushing ahead with the arms race was by spending millions of dollars on the Strategic Defense Initiative (SDI) project, commonly known as "Star Wars." This project involved the development of a powerful system designed to shoot down Soviet missiles before they reached the United States. Many experts considered the project impractical, too ex-

Mikhail and Raisa Gorbachev's daughter, Irina, attends a May Day parade with her daughter, Oksana, in Moscow's Red Square in 1985. May Day is celebrated each year in many countries to honor the workers of the world.

pensive, and probably impossible to develop. Reagan, however, chose to listen to others who argued in favor of the project.

Gorbachev considered SDI a major obstacle, in fact, a threat, to world peace. The development of such technology by the United States would make it necessary for the Soviet Union to counter with some advances of its own, and the intensity of the arms race would thereby increase rather than decrease. The Soviet Union could no longer afford to waste valuable rubles (Soviet money) on the military while so many Soviet people were hungry and jobless.

But Gorbachev's vision extended beyond the borders of the Soviet Union. He knew that if the world was going to have lasting peace, the arms race had to come to an end. And he understood that the world would be a better place once it began using its resources wisely instead of squandering them on a never-ending arms race.

In November 1985, Gorbachev met with Reagan in Geneva, Switzerland, to see what steps could be taken toward ending the arms race. However, the two men did not get their first meeting off to a very good start. To Reagan, the Soviet Union was an "evil empire" bent on world communism. To Gorbachev, Reagan was a product of the World War II era, incapable of seeing beyond the worn-out assumptions of the cold war. They argued over their countries' roles in the military conflicts in Nicaragua and Afghanistan. By the time they finally turned their attention to arms control, the two leaders were frustrated. At Gorbachev's suggestion that "fresh air may bring fresh ideas," the two leaders decided to take a walk outside.

Reagan then proposed that both nations reduce their nuclear weapons by half. Gorbachev was pleased, but then asked about SDI. On that matter, Reagan was firm: He could not give up the project. Gorbachev was also firm on SDI: As long as the United States insisted on developing SDI, there could be no agreement. They retired for the night having made little or no progress.

The next day, Reagan attacked Gorbachev on the issue of human rights. Despite the recent release of some Soviet political prisoners, there were many such prisoners still locked away in Soviet jails. Also, many Soviet citizens wished to leave the Soviet Union, even for brief periods, but were denied that privilege. Many Soviet Jews, for example, who wished to join members of their family in other countries were not allowed to do so. Reagan urged Gorbachev to free prisoners of conscience and to allow Soviet citizens to leave the Soviet Union if they wished to do so.

Gorbachev had no patience for Reagan's commentary on alleged Soviet human rights violations. Like the Soviet leaders before him, Gorbachev believed that the internal affairs of each country are that country's own business and are not open to foreign criticism. But, since Reagan had seen fit to level such criticism, Gorbachev did not hesitate to do the same. He reminded Reagan of the many hungry and homeless people in the United States, the number of which had drastically increased during the Reagan years. He asked whether Reagan considered access to food and shelter a basic human right and, if so, why he was allowing these to be denied in the United States, particularly while his government spent an increasing amount of money on military weapons.

Despite their differences and their heated arguments, Reagan and Gorbachev were eventually able to iron out a general agreement at the Geneva summit. They agreed to reduce nuclear weapons on both sides by half and also to renew educational, cultural, scientific, and athletic exchanges between their two countries. At their farewell dinner, the two superpower leaders raised their glasses in a toast to future agreements. The SDI issue had not been resolved, but the two leaders agreed to meet again soon and to work together toward peace.

Their next meeting took place in Reykjavik, Iceland, in October 1986. There, Gorbachev proposed further reduction of nuclear warheads beyond the one-half already agreed to. His sweep-

Gorbachev (front row, second from right) and other officials attend a gala performance at Moscow's Bolshoi Theater in March 1985. At the Geneva summit, Gorbachev and Reagan agreed to promote cultural exchanges between their two countries.

ing proposals stunned Reagan and his aides. When they recovered from their surprise, the Americans made a counterproposal. Then, Gorbachev raised the issue of SDI again. Reagan stuck to his guns on Star Wars, and Gorbachev refused to sign any agreement that allowed the United States to pursue the project. Once more, negotiations were deadlocked, and the two leaders parted without signing a treaty.

The world had watched the Reykjavik summit very closely, and when it was all over many were disappointed with the outcome. Following the summit, many people considered Gorbachev a bold innovator with vision who was willing to take risks and make sacrifices (as long as the United States did the same) for the sake of world peace. They considered Reagan a stubborn old cold-warrior, uninterested in reaching an agreement with the "evil empire." Others felt that, given the relative strength of the U.S. economy, Reagan was right to be firm with Gorbachev, who was seeking an agreement primarily for his country's economic well-being, as well as for his own political survival. In truth, both leaders had very good reasons to want an agreement between their two countries, and they were determined to get one. When Gorbachev left Geneva, he accepted Reagan's invitation to visit the United States.

On December 8, 1987, the Gorbachevs set foot on American soil, and before long, "Gorbymania" swept the nation. During a one-hour televised interview, Gorbachev was dazzling. He answered questions with intelligence and humor and quickly won over the American public and the media, which gave him the nickname "Gorby." He was greeted at the White House by a 21-gun salute.

This time, Reagan and Gorbachev were able to bridge many of the gaps they had between them. They continued to argue about Afghanistan, Nicaragua, Soviet Jews, the growing homeless population in American cities, and SDI. But eventually they reached a historic agreement eliminating an entire class of nuclear weapons, ceremoniously exchanging silver pens after each signed his translated copy of the treaty.

Afterward, there was a formal dinner at the White House to celebrate what was clearly a new day in U.S.-Soviet relations. Before Gorbachev left to return home, however, he extended an invitation to President Reagan and his wife, Nancy, to visit the Soviet Union the following year. The Reagans accepted.

In June 1988, Ronald and Nancy Reagan spent four days as Gorbachev's guests. They toured Red Square, the area outside the Kremlin walls in the center of Moscow. President Reagan, now 77 years old, spoke openly with the public and with members of the Soviet press. In Moscow, in the twilight of his presidency, Reagan was experiencing perhaps the greatest reward of his political career—the full knowledge that he and his administration had unexpectedly and dramatically improved relations between the world's superpowers.

Though the moment was sweet for him as well, Gorbachev had his whole career ahead of him and many challenges on the immediate horizon. In fact, for Gorbachev, only 57 years old, his greatest rewards were yet to come.

*President-elect George Bush, Reagan, and Gorbachev
visit Governor's Island in New York City in
December 1988. Reagan and Gorbachev forged strong
new bonds between the superpowers that would affect
world politics well into the future.*

6

The World
Will Be
Watching

The Gorbachevs returned to the United States
in December 1988. Though they loved the Gorbachevs as they love all celebrities, New Yorkers
had mixed feelings about the couple's upcoming
visit. New York is one huge traffic jam during the
winter holiday season, with long lines of Christ-
mas shoppers at the checkout counters and grid-
lock at every intersection. When the Gorbachevs
arrived on December 6 with their 45-car motorcade, some 6,000 police officers were assigned to
manage the heavy car and pedestrian traffic. New

Yorkers were quick to coin the term *Gorbilock*, referring to the hopeless traffic jams at city intersections caused by the crowds and by the closing of certain routes.

Gorbachev spoke at the United Nations on December 7 and shocked the General Assembly by announcing that the Soviet Union would drastically reduce the number of troops it had stationed in Eastern Europe. Some 500,000 men and 10,000 tanks would be withdrawn. Then he explained that the Soviet Union would make this move unilaterally, that is, without requiring the United States to make any similar reduction of its own. Next, he brought up the issue of human rights and promised to begin releasing political prisoners and issuing visas. Then, Gorbachev called for a cease-fire in Afghanistan effective January 1, 1989. The dramatic reform program Gorbachev outlined that day in New York showed the world that when it came to bringing about a lasting world peace, he meant business.

Gorbachev then boarded a ferry for Governors Island, where he would have lunch with President Reagan and President-elect George Bush. They enjoyed a gourmet meal and chatted like old friends. The luncheon was a far cry from their tense meeting in Geneva only three years before. After their meal and a brief look at the Statue of Liberty, the Gorbachevs went on a driving tour of the city.

As soon as the Soviet leader's motorcade entered the heart of New York's theater district—with throngs of well-wishers lining both sides of the street—Gorbachev was up to his old theatrics. In front of the Winter Garden Theatre, he ordered the driver to stop the car, got out, and began to greet the cheering crowd. "Gorby! Gorby!" they shouted as Gorbachev smiled broadly and moved toward them. He shook several hands, got back in the car on the advice of his KGB agents, and rode off. A bit later, Gorbachev pulled a similar stunt in front of a popular department store.

The Gorbachevs had planned to move on to Cuba and then Great Britain after visiting New York, but tragedy forced them to cancel their plans and return home. They received word that a severe earthquake had struck Armenia, one of the Soviet Union's 15 republics, killing some 25,000 people and injuring many more. His plane took off immediately from New York's Kennedy Airport.

Gorbachev arrived in Armenia to find the damage to lives and property much worse than anything he had expected. Realizing that the victims needed help fast, he sent out an international request for aid. Quickly, the goodwill that Gorbachev spread throughout the world paid off. Money and supplies came in from Great Britain, Japan, Israel, and other countries. The United States raised more than $3 million.

Gorbachev's handling of the Armenian earthquake crisis brought him world recognition because it showed that his style of leadership was dramatically different than that of previous Soviet leaders. It did this in two important ways.

First, it was surprising that Gorbachev would even consider asking for outside aid. Previous Soviet leaders usually denied that natural disasters happened in the Soviet Union or greatly downplayed the actual extent of the damage. By requesting aid, Gorbachev was saying that the Soviet Union no longer considered itself apart from the world community and that cooperation was important for the future of the world in both good and bad times.

Second, it was significant that news about the tragedy flowed freely throughout the Soviet Union and around the world. This was another result of Gorbachev's policy of openness. Foreign journalists were invited to cover the tragedy and were even allowed to enter some of the hardest-hit towns with television cameras. Unlike during the Stalin years, when a severe earthquake killed 100,000 people in the republic of Turkmen and hardly a word was uttered about it in the press, Gorbachev made sure the world was informed. Things were clearly different now. Now there was glasnost.

Glasnost has had its effect not only in the Soviet Union but on its neighbors as well. Seeing the dramatic changes within the Soviet Union, countries such as Poland, Czechoslovakia, Romania, East Germany, and Hungary—since World War II, dominated socially, politically, and economically by the Soviet Union—began to hunger for more freedom. Demonstrations in these countries quickly snowballed into a number of full-fledged movements for independence. And Gorbachev, in his wisdom, allowed these movements to gain momentum while urging caution.

In the past, Soviet leaders were not as tolerant. They sent troops into neighboring countries to stop freedom and democracy from taking root in Eastern Europe. For example, Soviet troops invaded Hungary in 1956, when the people of that nation rose up to declare their independence. Also, in 1968, Soviet forces invaded Czechoslovakia during a brief period known as Prague Spring, when the Czech people, led by Alexander Dubček, tried to free themselves from Soviet rule.

Instead of using violence to force so-called satellite states to remain in the grip of communism, Gorbachev has been more inclined to allow history to take its course. In fact, some 20 years later, Gorbachev's glasnost bears a striking resemblance to Dubček's "socialism with a human face." For Gorbachev, *glasnost* is not just a word, it is a principle of justice and a historical necessity.

As the movement toward freedom and democracy continued to sweep through Eastern Europe, Communist party conservatives became increasingly dissatisfied. They believed Gorbachev's glasnost was being taken too far, and they had added proof when the small republics on the eastern border of the Soviet Union—the Baltic states—began to behave like the independence-seeking countries of Eastern Europe. In the republics of Latvia, Estonia, and Lithuania, all under Soviet rule since 1940, there were calls for greater independence from Moscow. Party conservatives feared that the Soviet Union might fall apart piece by piece.

The party conservatives were not the only ones unhappy with Gorbachev. Many Soviet citizens, having seen very little improvement in the Soviet economy since Gorbachev began his reform program, became impatient with Gorbachev as the 1990s began. Despite perestroika and a certain degree of progress, Soviet businesses continued to fail. Consumer goods remained widely unavailable or very expensive, and adequate housing was increasingly difficult to find. Farmers struggled to survive, and long lines formed for

In his first few years as Soviet leader, Gorbachev improved his country's image abroad and paved the way for political debate within its borders. But with the Soviet economy in shambles, Gorbachev's greatest challenges lie ahead.

even such basics as bread and potatoes. The country's morale continued to sink. During the mid-1980s, the Soviet people were hopeful and enthusiastic; as the 1990s began, they were anxious and worried.

Gorbachev never said he would work miracles. Though he has acted quickly and boldly, he has also stressed the need for patience. The Soviet economy is in such bad shape that it will take many years before it can recover fully. It is Gorbachev's hope that perestroika will give the Soviet people the opportunity to turn the economy around and that the spirit of glasnost will encourage the Soviet people to speak and act freely and to be creative in their thinking. In general, Gorbachev hopes that his reforms will inspire the Soviet people to make a better life for themselves. He cannot do it for them. Whether his bold reforms will make it possible for them to forge meaningful and productive lives for themselves remains to be seen. Whatever happens, the world will be watching.

Chronology

March 2, 1931	Mikhail Sergeevich Gorbachev born in Privolnoye in Stavropol, USSR
1941	Germany invades the Soviet Union
1945	World War II ends; Gorbachev joins the Komsomol
1950–55	Gorbachev studies law at Moscow State University
1952	Accepted into the Communist party
1954	Marries Raisa Titorenko
1955	Returns to Stavropol and takes position as deputy chief of propaganda of the local Komsomol
1958	Named first secretary of the Stavropol regional Komsomol
1970	Appointed first secretary of the Communist party for the Stavropol region
1971	Named a member of the Central Committee of the Communist party of the Soviet Union
1978	Becomes Central Committee agricultural secretary

1980	Promoted to full membership in the Politburo
1982	Yuri Andropov becomes the leader of the Soviet Union
1984	Andropov dies; Konstantin Chernenko becomes the Soviet leader
March 1985	Chernenko dies; Gorbachev becomes the general secretary of the Communist party and leader of the Soviet Union
Nov. 1985	Summit meeting with U.S. president Reagan in Geneva, Switzerland; The U.S. and the Soviet Union agree to reduce nuclear weapons on both sides by half
April 25, 1986	Accident at the Chernobyl nuclear power plant in the Ukraine
1986	Gorbachev releases a number of political prisoners, including Anatoly Scharansky and Andrei Sakharov
Oct. 1986	Summit meeting with President Reagan in Reykjavik, Iceland; dispute over SDI causes a deadlock in the negotiations
Dec. 1987	The Gorbachevs visit the United States; Gorbachev and Reagan reach

	an agreement eliminating an entire class of nuclear weapons
Dec. 1988	At the UN, Gorbachev announces a planned unilateral reduction in Soviet troops stationed in Eastern Europe; Armenian earthquake kills thousands on December 9; Gorbachev returns to the Soviet Union to manage the disaster
1989	Glasnost stirs a movement for democracy and independence throughout Eastern Europe, and the Communisty party's monopoly on power in Poland, Hungary, Bulgaria, East Germany, Czechoslovakia, and Romania comes to an end
1990	Gorbachev is under increasing pressure as the Soviet economy continues to fail; political factions within the Soviet Union question Gorbachev's effectiveness and urge him to share power; Gorbachev wins Nobel Peace Prize in October

Glossary

arms control a program that restricts the production of nuclear weapons

arms race the escalation in the production of nuclear weapons between the United States and the Soviet Union

black market trade in goods that violates official regulations

capitalism an economic system based on competition and private ownership of the means of production

closed society a society in which political participation, travel, and the public expression of opinion are strictly regulated by the government

cold war the term used to describe the shifting struggle for power and prestige between the Western powers and the Communist bloc from the end of World War II until the early 1990s

communism an economic system based on common ownership of the means of production and an equal distribution of wealth

dissident a person who publicly expresses disapproval of government policies or actions

exile the expulsion of a person from his or her country by the government

glasnost   the Russian word for "openness"; refers to changes initiated by Gorbachev to encourage public debate

KGB   the Soviet Union's police force

Komsomol (Communist Youth League)   a group dedicated to preparing young men and women for membership in the Communist party

Kremlin   the fortress in Moscow that houses the Soviet government

nuclear weapon   a weapon that gains its destructive energy from the splitting (fission) or union (fusion) of atomic nuclei

passport   a government-issued document that allows a person to travel to a foreign country

perestroika   a Russian word meaning "restructuring"; refers to Gorbachev's goals for restructuring the economic and political system of the Soviet Union as well as the way in which countries relate to each other

Politburo   the Soviet Union's ruling government body

political prisoners   prisoners of conscience; people jailed for holding political beliefs in opposition to those of the government

propaganda   the manipulation of ideas, media reports, and rumors in order to help or harm an institution, group, or person

revolution the overthrow of a government by its citizens

satellite state a country dominated socially, politically, and economically by a more powerful country

secret service the division of the United States Treasury Department charged with the protection of the president and foreign dignitaries and rulers as well as with the suppression of counterfeiting

serf a hired laborer who plants and harvests crops for a landlord in return for protection, housing, and a portion of the crop

socialism an economic system in which there is government ownership of the means of production and distribution of goods; thought by Karl Marx to be a transition stage between capitalism and communism

Strategic Defense Initiative SDI; Star Wars; a project for shooting down enemy missiles while they are still on course

summit a conference of high-level government officials

treaty an agreement in writing between two or more countries

United Nations UN; a worldwide organization of independent nations, founded in 1945, after World War II, to promote international peace and cooperation

John W. Selfridge is an editor and a freelance writer with a special interest in 20th-century history and culture. He holds an M.A. from Columbia University, where he studied literature, philosophy, and education, and has consulted on more than 100 books for young adults. He is the author of several biographies for young readers.